Contents

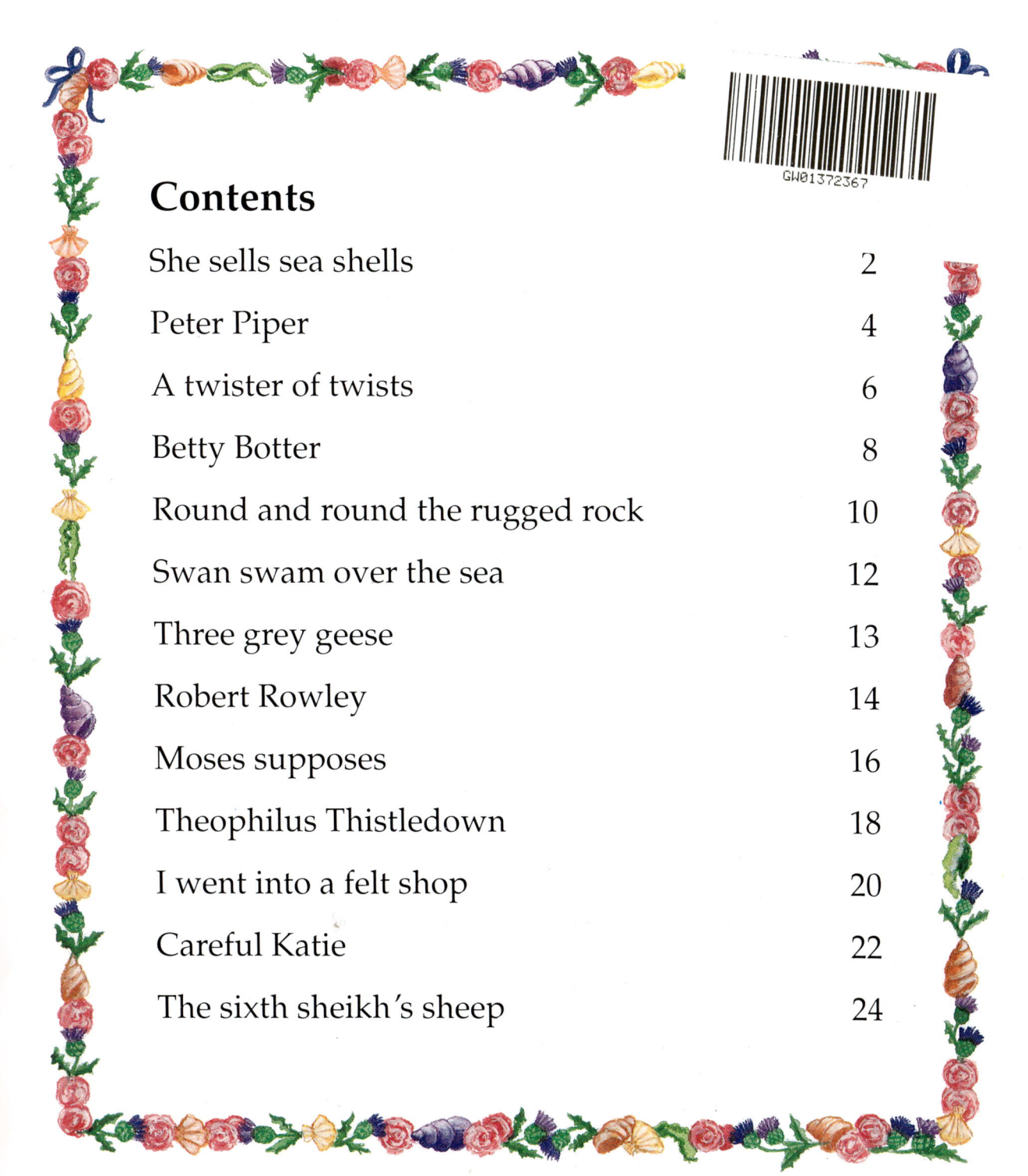

She sells sea shells	2
Peter Piper	4
A twister of twists	6
Betty Botter	8
Round and round the rugged rock	10
Swan swam over the sea	12
Three grey geese	13
Robert Rowley	14
Moses supposes	16
Theophilus Thistledown	18
I went into a felt shop	20
Careful Katie	22
The sixth sheikh's sheep	24

She sells sea-shells on the sea shore;
The sea shells that she sells are sea-shells I'm sure.
So if she sells sea-shells on the sea shore,
I'm sure that the shells are sea-shore shells.

3

Peter Piper picked a peck of pickled pepper;
Did Peter Piper pick a peck of pickled pepper?
If Peter Piper picked a peck of pickled pepper.
Where's the peck of pickled pepper Peter Piper picked?

5

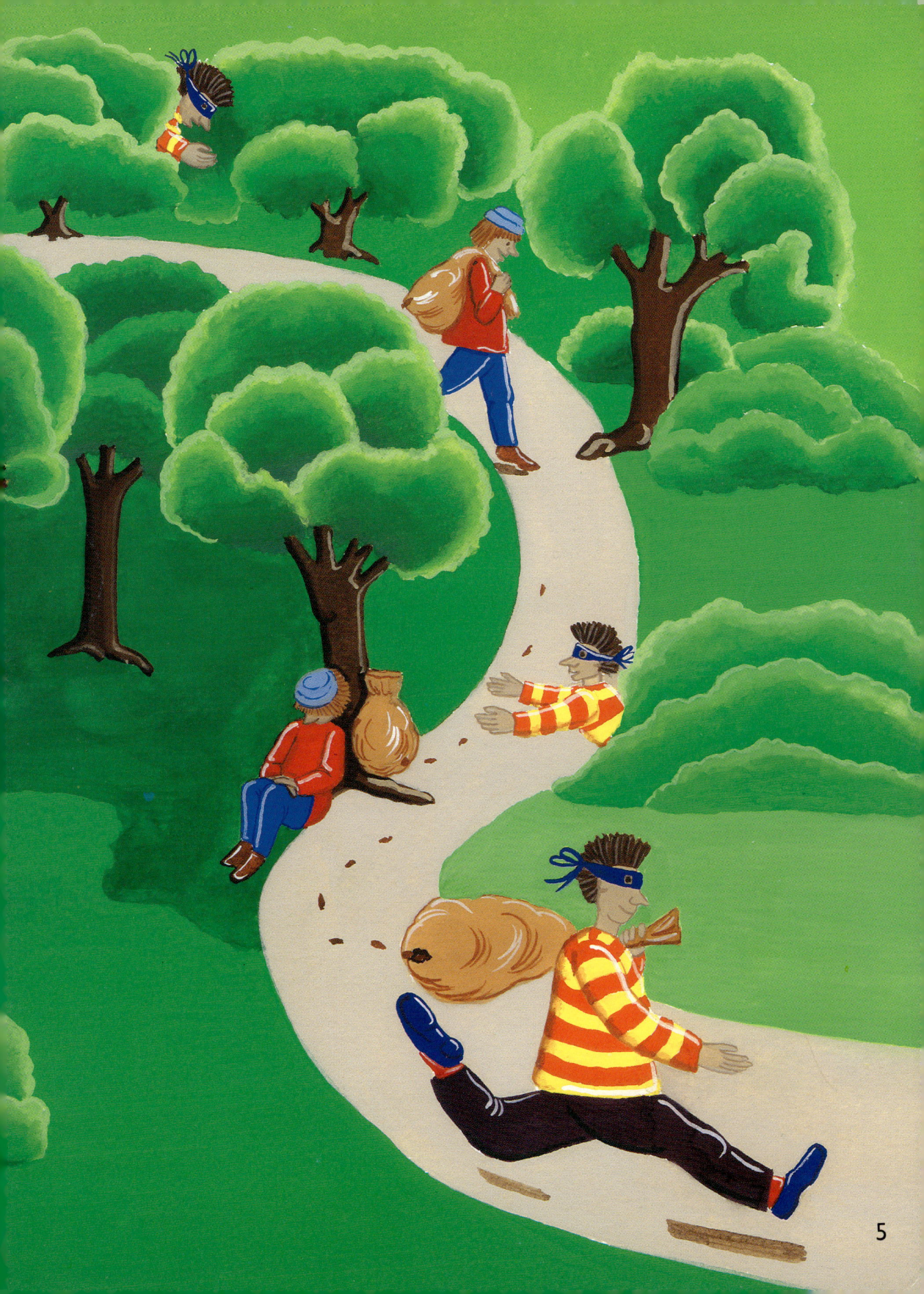

A twister of twists once twisted a twist,
The twist that he twisted was a twisted twist;
If in twisting the twist, one twist should untwist,
The untwisted twist would untwist the twist.

7

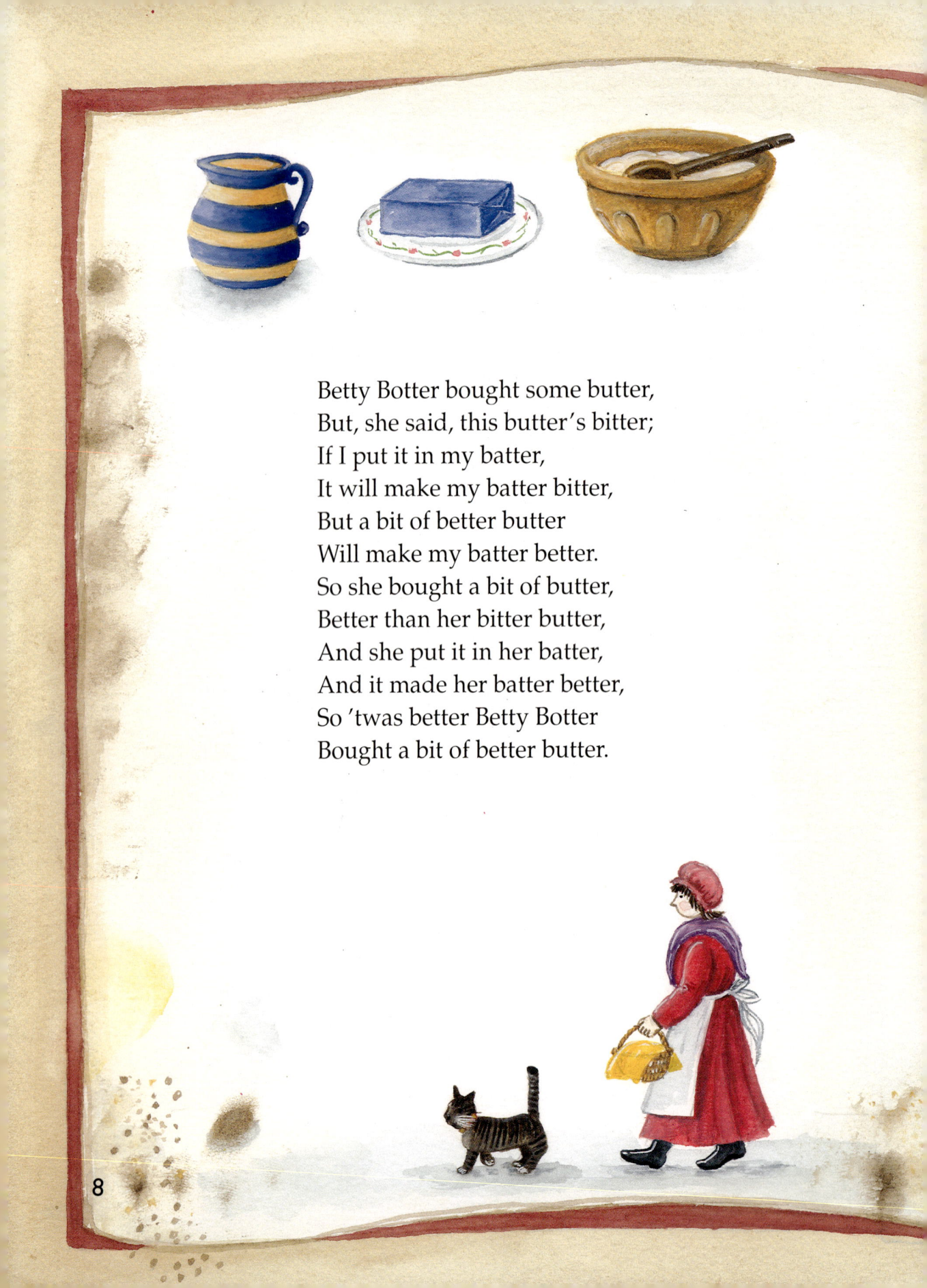

Betty Botter bought some butter,
But, she said, this butter's bitter;
If I put it in my batter,
It will make my batter bitter,
But a bit of better butter
Will make my batter better.
So she bought a bit of butter,
Better than her bitter butter,
And she put it in her batter,
And it made her batter better,
So 'twas better Betty Botter
Bought a bit of better butter.

9

Round and round the rugged rock the ragged rascal ran

How many R's are there in THAT? Now tell me if you can.

Swan swam over the sea,
Swim swan swim!
Swan swam back again
Well swum swan!

Three grey geese
in a green field grazing,
Grey were the geese
and green was the grazing.

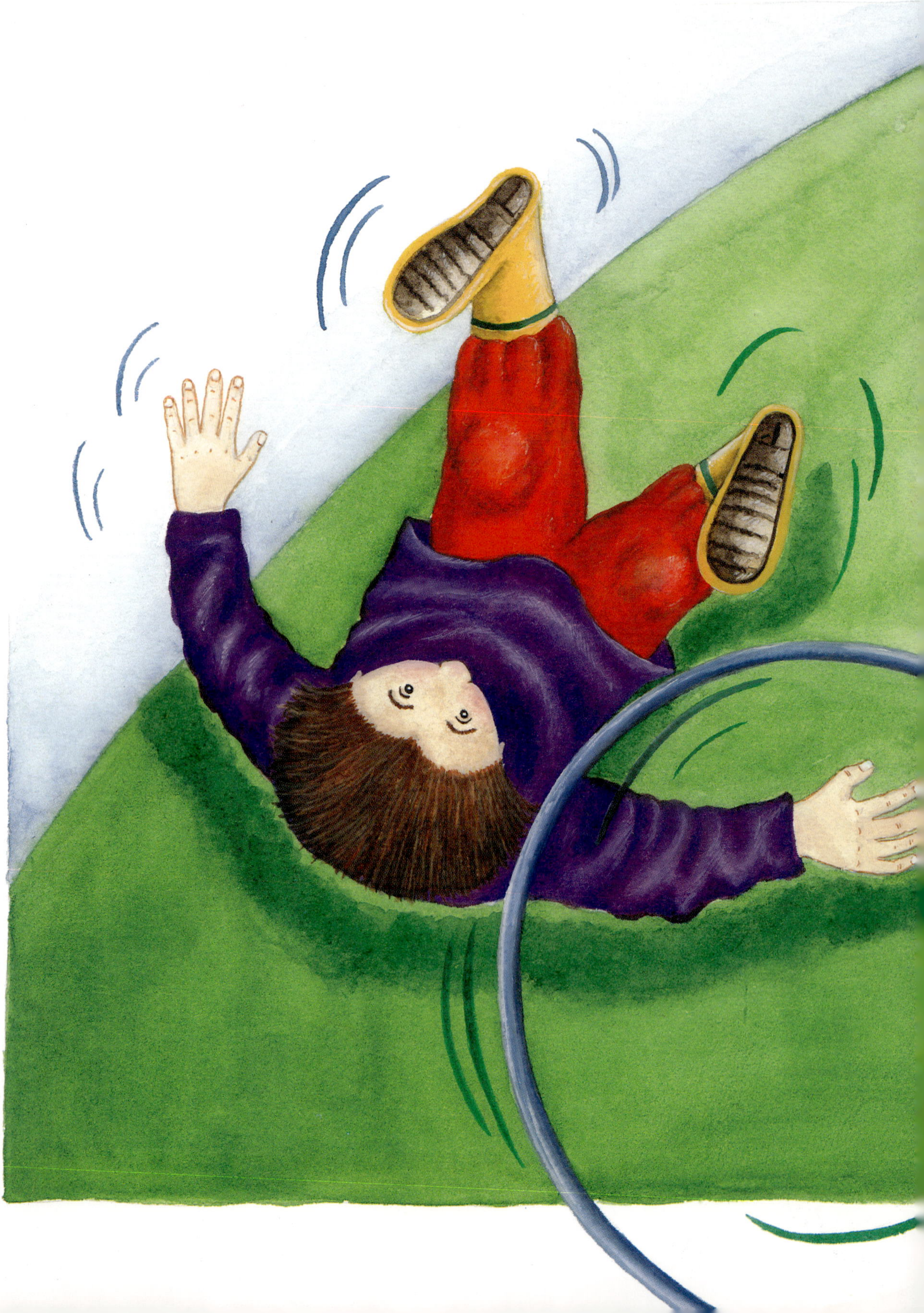

Robert Rowley rolled a round roll round,
A round roll Robert Rowley rolled round;
Where rolled the round roll
Robert Rowley rolled round?

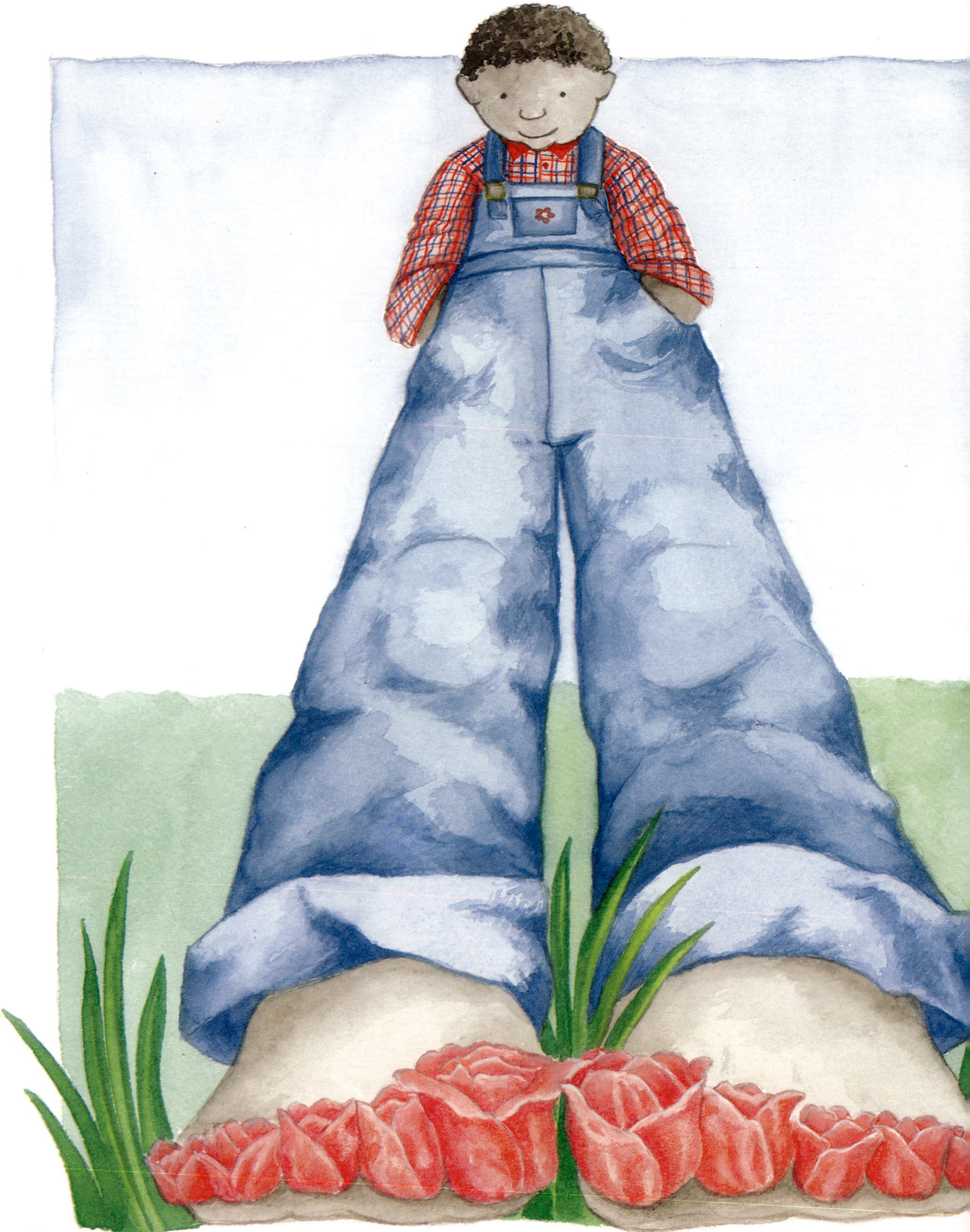

Moses supposes his toeses are roses,
But Moses supposes erroneously;
For nobody's toeses are posies of roses
As Moses supposes his toeses to be.

Theophilus Thistledown, the successful thistle sifter,
in sifting a sieve of unsifted thistles,
thrust three thousand thistles
through the thick of his thumb.

19

I went into a felt shop
and felt a piece of felt
of all the felt I've ever felt
I never felt a piece of felt
that felt like that felt felt!

21

Careful Katie cooked a crisp and crinkly cabbage;
Did careful Katie cook a crisp and crinkly cabbage?
If careful Katie cooked a crisp and crinkly cabbage,
Where's the crisp and crinkly cabbage
Careful Katie cooked?

23

24